Original title:
Smoky Eddies Above the Phoenix Mull

Author: Sebastian Sarapuu
ISBN HARDBACK: 978-1-80563-365-5
ISBN PAPERBACK: 978-1-80564-886-4

Whispers of Time Beneath Shimmering Waves

In twilight's embrace, the water glows,
Whispers of secrets, where the soft wind blows.
The tides intertwine with the stories of old,
Hidden in shadows, tales yet untold.

Stars twinkle above in a sapphire sky,
Guiding the dreams as the night drifts by.
Each ripple sings softly, a hymn of the past,
Carrying echoes of moments that last.

Beneath the surface, where the silence reigns,
Lives a world of magic, unchained by the pains.
Creatures of wonder, in the depths they dance,
Spinning their stories in a timeless trance.

Whispers grow louder, as dawn's light breaks,
Painting the waters in golden wakes.
Promises linger, like grains of soft sand,
Forever entwined in time's gentle hand.

In laughter and sorrow, the currents flow,
Embracing the moments that ebb and grow.
For in every wave, a memory lies,
A treasure of life, beneath endless skies.

Enigmatic Flames Amongst the Currents

In twilight's glow, where shadows dance,
Flames flicker brightly, a spellbound glance.
Currents entwined with whispers of fire,
Igniting the dreams of those who aspire.

A flicker of gold in the midnight blue,
Sparks fly like stars as their secrets are true.
Amongst the chaos, in hearts that ignite,
Burns the desire, a mystical light.

With every movement, the flames sway and spin,
In a ballet of passion, where stories begin.
Dancing through shadows, they paint the night sky,
Radiant echoes that never say die.

Enigmas entwined in the heat of the flame,
Each spark holds a story, each flicker a name.
As embers whisper of tales never told,
A canvas of warmth, in the dark, bold.

As dawn approaches, the flames flicker low,
Yet deep in the current, their magic will flow.
For even in silence, their wisdom will gleam,
A tapestry woven from hope and from dream.

Veiled Flames of Forgotten Histories

In the dark where shadows creep,
Old stories whisper, secrets deep.
Veiled flames dance with ghostly light,
Revealing tales lost to the night.

Beneath the ashes, embers glow,
Time's tapestry begins to flow.
Heroes rise from silent sleep,
As ancient promises weep.

A flicker of truths long concealed,
A tapestry slowly revealed.
With each breath, the past ignites,
A tapestry of lost delights.

So gather close 'neath starlit skies,
Hear the echoes as history sighs.
In the veiled flames, we find our way,
To forgotten realms where shadows play.

Flickers of Twilight on Liquid Realms

Flickers dance on water's face,
Twilight's embrace, a gentle grace.
Rippling dreams in colors bright,
Twilight weaves the day's last light.

Whispers call from depths unseen,
In the stillness, the world serene.
Liquid realms of shimmering gold,
Where stories of old are retold.

The moon dips low, a silver key,
Unlocking magic from the sea.
On this canvas, brushstrokes glide,
Each flicker holds a world inside.

As the stars awaken and twirl,
In liquid realms, our visions swirl.
Flickers of twilight, soft and fair,
Guide our thoughts to places rare.

Murmurs of the River's Everlasting Dance

Murmurs rise from waters clear,
Timeless tunes that draw us near.
The river flows, a gentle sigh,
Carrying dreams beneath the sky.

Each ripple tells a tale anew,
Of whispered secrets, old and true.
Beneath the waves, the echoes play,
The river's dance will never sway.

In moonlit nights, the waters gleam,
Reflecting hopes, a flowing dream.
With every turn, the waters wend,
A journey that knows no end.

Murmurs soft as summer rain,
Invite the heart to feel its strain.
In the river's timeless trance,
We learn to trust its sweet romance.

Forgotten Essences in the Tide's Song

In the ebb, where whispers dwell,
Forgotten essences might tell.
The tide's song hums of days long past,
A melody of shadows cast.

Shells and stories intertwine,
Nature's brush on sands divine.
Each wave a note, a tale it sings,
Of ancient days, and forgotten things.

Dancing light on liquid paths,
Evoking laughter, mingled with baths.
Though time may fade and memory stall,
The tide remembers, embracing all.

In whispers soft, the essences rise,
Stirring reflection 'neath twilight skies.
Listen closely, let your heart belong,
To the tide's eternal, soothing song.

Shadowed Moments on the Edge of Darkness

In whispers low, the shadows creep,
The twilight breathes, where secrets sleep.
Beneath the moon's soft, silvery glow,
Lies a world hidden, wrapped in woe.

Voices carried by the night's soft breeze,
Echo tales of forgotten leaves.
Time ticks softly, a lingering sigh,
As the stars weave dreams through the sky.

Pale figures dance in the shroud of gray,
Lost in stories of forgotten days.
Each step a memory, a shattered spark,
Guiding souls through the depths of dark.

A moment captured, yet fleeting fast,
Fading echoes that whisper the past.
In silence thick, we brace the fall,
For in the dark, we find it all.

So linger here, where the shadows play,
And embrace the night in its haunting way.
For even in darkness, there's light to see,
In shadowed moments, we find the key.

Resonance of Memories in Flowing Tides

The ocean hums a lullaby sweet,
Waves crash softly, a rhythmic beat.
In each ripple lies a tale untold,
Of lovers parting and giants bold.

Seagulls cry where the waters rush,
Whispers of time in the ocean's hush.
Shells scattered like dreams on the shore,
Each one a memory, a whispered lore.

As tide pulls back, the sand reveals,
Footprints marking how time steals.
With every ebb, stories arise,
Of distant lands and endless skies.

In flowing tides, we find our place,
In a dance with time, a tender embrace.
Each wave a heartbeat, each swell a sigh,
Fitful moments drift by like the sky.

Let the currents carry you gently through,
To where past and present blend anew.
For in these tides, memories reside,
In resonance deep, where love can't hide.

Silken Threads in the River's Fabric

In a river deep, where silence sings,
Silken threads weave timeless things.
Golden glimmers catch the light,
As the current dances, soft and bright.

Among the reeds, whispers play,
Secrets told, then washed away.
In the flow, old tales are spun,
Of battles fought and victories won.

Each ripple carries a note of grace,
Tracing history, a gentle embrace.
With every turn, the waters flow,
A tapestry rich, where dreams bestow.

Time intertwines in the river's seam,
Life like a river, fleeting as dream.
Yet in the fabric, hope is sewn,
In silken threads, we're never alone.

So let your heart drift, unconfined,
In the river's weave, your soul entwined.
For in its depths, the stories glow,
Like silken threads in the ebb and flow.

Flickering Veils in the Gloom of Night

Beneath the shroud of twilight's grace,
Flickering veils dance, a ghostly trace.
In shadows deep, secrets are sown,
In the quiet gloom, we're not alone.

The stars above, like lanterns bright,
Guide the lost through the depth of night.
Each flicker carries a promise near,
A whisper sweet for all who hear.

Winds carry tales of ancient lore,
Cloaked in dreams forevermore.
In every rustle, a sigh can be found,
Echoes of heartbeats, soft and profound.

Veils of mist, a soft refrain,
Caress the earth like gentle rain.
With each step taken, we seek to know,
The flickered paths where lost things go.

So let the night wrap you tight,
In its arms of shadows, hidden from sight.
For though it may seem dark and trite,
There's beauty found in the gloom of night.

Whispers of the Ashen Skies

In the hush of twilight's sigh,
Where shadows gently fold,
Soft whispers weave a lullaby,
Of secrets yet untold.

Beneath the clouds of smoky gray,
Dreams drift on the breeze,
Each thought a fleeting wisp of day,
Lost in endless seas.

Faint echoes through the dusky air,
Call out to those who roam,
With every breath, a silent prayer,
To guide the wanderers home.

As stars begin to pierce the night,
Their twinkle dances free,
In the silence, there's pure delight,
A dance of memory.

The ash-streaked skies, a canvas wide,
With tales of years gone by,
In every gust, the worlds collide,
As whispers softly fly.

Currents of Faded Remnants

In the river's gentle flow,
Memories intertwine,
Currents carry tales of woe,
And spark of lost design.

Leaves that float like dreams at rest,
In the stillness, gleam,
Whispering of natures' best,
And time's elusive theme.

Stone bridges arch with grace and age,
Over waters deep,
Each ripple writes a timeless page,
In the heart we keep.

Ghosts of laughter dance along,
Beneath the willow's sway,
In faded remnants, life's sweet song,
Finds its own way to play.

So let the current sweep away,
The sorrows of the past,
For in each drop, a chance to stay,
And make the moment last.

Embracing the Embered Breeze

Amidst the glow of fading light,
The evening whispers soft,
A tender breeze takes gentle flight,
As shadows lift aloft.

Embers flicker, warm and bright,
In hearts that seek a fire,
Each spark ignites the starry night,
With dreams that will inspire.

Through fields of gold where wildflowers sway,
The dusk begins to hum,
In every petal, life's ballet,
Reveals what's yet to come.

The air is thick with stories spun,
Of battles fought and won,
As twilight sings, the day is done,
The night has just begun.

Embrace the breeze, a lover's call,
As it wraps you up tight,
In every breath, let shadows fall,
And dance into the night.

Shadows Danced in the Twilight

As day bids night a soft adieu,
The shadows start to sing,
In twilight's grace, the world anew,
Awaits the night's gentle wing.

Figures sway beneath the trees,
In secret, soft ballet,
Dancing to the whispered breeze,
Evoking shades of gray.

With each flicker of the light,
Life's stories intertwine,
In the stillness of the night,
Silence draws the line.

Echoes of the day retreat,
As stars ignite the sky,
In twilight's arms, the heart feels beat,
With dreams that softly fly.

So let the shadows twirl and play,
In hues of dark and bright,
For in this dance, we find our way,
From twilight into night.

Tales Carried by the Wandering Wind

In whispered tones the stories grow,
Of ancient lands where magic flows.
The winds that weave through trees and glades,
Bring secrets rich where memory wades.

They speak of knights and dragons bold,
Of shimmering gems and treasures old.
A flicker here, a rustle there,
Imagination dances in the air.

Beneath the stars, the tales unite,
A tapestry spun in silvery light.
Each breath of breeze a passing thought,
In every corner, enchantments sought.

The wandering wind, it knows no bounds,
It carries hopes from distant grounds.
For every heart that longs to see,
The magic that can truly be.

Listen closely, heed its call,
For in its song, the dreams can sprawl.
Together we'll chase the veils of night,
When tales are born in the soft twilight.

Dances of Light Over Shaded Waters

Upon the lake where willows weep,
A dance of light begins to creep.
Each ripple holds a secret glint,
As shadows weave where dreams imprint.

The fireflies twirl in silken flight,
Painting whispers in the night.
Their glow reveals a hidden lore,
Of twinkling stars that ever soar.

Beneath the boughs where silence hums,
The heart of night so gently drums.
Reflecting hues on water's skin,
As magic stirs the depths within.

In twilight's breath, the world unfolds,
A canvas vast, a story told.
Lights pirouette on shrouded shores,
Each glimmer sings of myths and more.

So linger here, let time unwind,
In dances bright that fate designed.
For every glance upon this sea,
The light will guide you, wild and free.

Elysian Mists in Shadows of Dawn

As morning breaks, the mists arise,
Like whispered dreams in painted skies.
A gentle touch, a soft embrace,
Awakens life in this sacred space.

The world transforms with gilded hues,
Each shadow doused in dew-kissed blues.
In silence swells the day's first light,
A heralding of hope, so bright.

Elysian mists, they swirl and weave,
Unraveling secrets we hardly conceive.
In this moment, time stands still,
As wonder fills the quiet hill.

Birds take flight, their chorus sings,
A symphony of early things.
With every note, the heavens wake,
And in this charm, our fears forsake.

Let every dawn be cherished deep,
With mists that promise dreams to keep.
In shades of gold, the heart shall find,
A world reborn, a soul aligned.

Chasing Echoes of Fading Light

In twilight's grasp, the echoes call,
With whispers low that start to fall.
A serenade from distant days,
Where memories dance in sunset's blaze.

Chasing streaks of fading glow,
We wander paths where shadows grow.
The stories linger on the breeze,
As stars emerge, beneath the trees.

Each flicker tells of journeys past,
Of laughter shared and shadows cast.
In every pulse of night's embrace,
A stitch of time in twilight's grace.

The echoes lead, a haunting tune,
While starlight breathes beneath the moon.
Following dreams that drift away,
In fragile strands of yesterday.

So chase the light through veils unclear,
Embrace the dusk, let go of fear.
For in each echo, hope ignites,
A new beginning, chasing lights.

Labyrinthine Mists Over Shadowed Waters

In twilight's grasp, the mists do weave,
A path unclear, where shadows cleave.
Whispers dance on waters cold,
Where secrets lie, and tales unfold.

The silent swirls, like ghosts at play,
Guide weary souls who drift astray.
What lies beyond this veiled embrace?
A hidden truth, a lost place's trace.

A shimmer lingers, haunting bright,
In depths unknown, far from the light.
Echoes murmur through reeds that sway,
Inviting dreams to drift away.

Horizon Flames in Secrets of the Night

The horizon glows with embers bright,
A dance of flames in the cloak of night.
Secrets whispered on the breeze,
Unlocking hearts, tempting with ease.

As stars emerge, a shimmering shroud,
The world slumbers, soft and proud.
Each spark ignites forgotten dreams,
Beneath the moon, where magic streams.

In shadows deep, the spirits twine,
Their laughter light, a silver line.
In this realm, where wild hearts soar,
The night unveils what was before.

Elysium's Breath in the Drift of Time

Beneath the sky, where roses bloom,
Elysium's breath dispels all gloom.
A gentle touch upon the skin,
Awakens dreams once locked within.

In every breeze, a memory stirs,
A timeless dance, where silence purrs.
Each moment sways like petals cast,
In the embrace of a fading past.

Through corridors of whispered sighs,
The echoes linger, soft goodbyes.
In twilight's hue, the souls confide,
In Elysium's breath, we turn with pride.

Floating Dreams on the Liquid Canvas

Upon the lake, where dreams reside,
A liquid canvas, serene and wide.
With every ripple, a thought takes flight,
In vivid hues, on the edge of night.

Each brush of wind sends whispers bright,
Inwoven tales of lost delight.
The colors blend, like laughter's spell,
Inviting hearts where memories dwell.

Through shimmering waves, hopes gently glide,
As present dances with dreams inside.
Painting the air with souls so free,
Floating dreams, on a timeless sea.

Secret Flames in the Heart of the River

Beneath the whispering willow's shade,
A secret flame in waters laid.
It flickers soft, a ghostly glow,
Where wishes drift and sorrows flow.

Each ripple holds a fleeting spark,
In twilight's grace, a chance to hark.
The river's song, a gentle hum,
Calls forth the dreams that dare to come.

Within the depths, the spirits twine,
Weaving tales with threads divine.
A heart enshrined in watery grace,
In every ebb, a hidden place.

From roots of ancient trees, they rise,
With laughter twinkling 'neath the skies.
Those secret flames that flicker bright,
Guide lost souls through the velvet night.

So cast your fears upon the stream,
Let secret flames ignite your dream.
For in the heart of the river clear,
Awaits a world that draws you near.

Haunting Glimmers of Silvered Dreams

In shadows deep where whispers dwell,
Light dances soft, a farewell bell.
Silvered dreams on moonbeams ride,
Across the lake, where secrets bide.

Each star a spark of longing's tale,
A haunting glimmer in the pale.
The night unveils its mystic lore,
As hearts entwined forever soar.

Echoes linger where silence gleams,
In the essence of our dreams.
The silver threads of fate entwine,
To weave a tapestry divine.

Beneath the stars, the night does sing,
Of ancient hopes that dreams may bring.
With every pulse, a wish takes flight,
In haunting glimmers of the night.

So hold your breath, embrace the glow,
Let silvered dreams with whispers flow.
For in the darkness, light will bloom,
A haunting song dispels the gloom.

Aetherial Ghosts in the Silent Flow

In stillness where the waters lie,
Aetherial ghosts begin to sigh.
They glide like mist on moonlit tide,
In silent flow, their secrets hide.

With tender grace, they softly weave,
The tales of those who dare believe.
Through liquid realms, they twirl and spin,
A gentle dance where dreams begin.

Each wave a whisper of the past,
In fading light, their shadows cast.
They beckon forth the brave and bold,
To join their waltz in currents cold.

Amidst the ripples, hope unfolds,
A tapestry of stories told.
Aetherial echoes in the night,
Guide wandering hearts toward the light.

So let your spirit drift and roam,
In silent flows, you'll find your home.
For in each ghostly, fleeting breath,
Lies life anew in shades of death.

Timidity of Colors in the Veiled Stream

In the gentle bend of nature's grace,
Timid colors find their place.
With strokes of gold and hints of blue,
The veiled stream whispers secrets true.

Soft petals flutter, shy and frail,
In shimmering light, they tell their tale.
Each hue a note in nature's song,
Yet timid, where they feel they belong.

The emerald ferns embrace the shore,
While petals dance, and colors soar.
In quiet spaces where shadows blend,
Timidity keeps them as friends.

Through whispers low and breezes slight,
The colors blossom into the night.
In every ripple, dreams take flight,
A dance of shades in muted light.

So flow along the gentle stream,
Embrace the colors born from dream.
For in their shyness, beauty lies,
A tender heart beneath the skies.

Celestial Flames Woven in the Fog

In shadows cast by twilight's glow,
The stars dance high, a secret show.
With whispered light, they weave the night,
Celestial flames, so warm, so bright.

Through swirling mists, the spirits soar,
They hum a tune we can't ignore.
Each flicker tells the tales of old,
Of dreams once lost and hearts so bold.

As dawn creeps in with gentle grace,
The fog retreats, begins to trace.
A fleeting glimpse, a soft embrace,
Of memories time cannot erase.

Beneath the veil of night they dance,
These flames of hope, they hold a chance.
With every spark, a wish takes flight,
In harmony, they guide the night.

So heed the call of ancient skies,
In silent whispers, truth shall rise.
For in the fog, where shadows play,
Celestial flames light the way.

Lost Voices Beneath the Whispering Waves

In the embrace of the ocean's sigh,
Echoes of dreams in currents lie.
Each whispered voice, a tale untold,
Dances with the tides, so fierce, so bold.

Beneath the surface, the stories dwell,
Of sailors lost, and lovers' swell.
The moonlight drapes a silver shroud,
Where secrets linger, soft and loud.

The salt-kissed breeze carries their song,
A haunting tune where shadows throng.
With every wave, a memory stirs,
Of heartache's grief and laughter's purrs.

Through depths of blue, a longing flows,
For those who seek the light that glows.
In whispers soft, the ocean shares,
The lost voices caught in its cares.

So listen well to the waters' heart,
As they weave tales, a work of art.
Beneath the waves, where spirits play,
Their echoing love shall never sway.

Shrouded Tales in the Flowing Mist

In morning's haze, the world is still,
A canvas drawn with nature's will.
Shrouded tales in mist's embrace,
Where dreams entwine in softest grace.

The trees stand tall, the shadows creep,
Guardians of secrets, silent deep.
With every fog that blankets land,
Stories rise like grains of sand.

Voices murmur, soft as breath,
Of love and loss, of life and death.
In tender swirls, their whispers dance,
Invoking hope, a fateful chance.

Through tendrils thick, the past reveals,
The magic spun, the heart that heals.
In flowing mist, a journey starts,
Where every tale is spun from hearts.

So wander forth through veils of grey,
Where shadows play and spirits sway.
In every sigh, a legend's kiss,
Embrace the shroud, and find your bliss.

Echoes of Dawn Amidst Whispered Currents

As dawn awakes with gentle light,
The shadows fade, abandoning night.
Echoes of dreams in colors bright,
Whispered currents take their flight.

Through golden rays, the world ignites,
Reflecting hope in morning's sights.
Each ripple sings a brand-new song,
Of paths anew where we belong.

The river flows with stories shared,
Of hearts once lost and souls laid bare.
In every glance, the past remains,
A tapestry of joys and pains.

With soft caress, the waters glide,
Carrying dreams on the rising tide.
As echoes swirl and softly blend,
They herald change, where journeys end.

So greet the dawn, let spirits soar,
In whispered currents, we'll explore.
With every heartbeat, life unfolds,
Echoes of dawn, a tale retold.

Veils of Mist Over Ancient Waters

In the hush where shadows speak,
Veils of mist in silence creep.
Across the waters, secrets flow,
Echoing tales of long ago.

Ghostly forms drift to and fro,
Kissed by moonlight's gentle glow.
Whispered dreams in soft embrace,
In this realm, we find our place.

Ripples dance on surface clear,
Carrying whispers for the ear.
Ancient voices rise anew,
In the depths, the old feels true.

Murmurs linger in the air,
Each breath filled with twilight's care.
Secrets guarded, holding tight,
Veils of mist conceal the night.

With each dawn, the tales return,
For in the heart, the embers burn.
Through the mists, life's story weaves,
An eternal thread that believes.

Whispers in the Twilight Currents

As the dusk begins to fall,
Softest whispers seem to call.
Currents twirl with lessons learned,
In the twilight, wisdom earned.

Shadows stretch and then recede,
Nature's pulse in rustling creed.
Crickets chirp their evening song,
In this world, we all belong.

Rippling waters softly weave,
Magic lingers, do not leave.
Fingers touch the surface bare,
In this moment, peace is rare.

Lanterns flicker, stars ignite,
Guiding souls through the night.
Each heartbeat in gentle flow,
Carried forth where dreams may go.

In the currents, hearts entwined,
Through the dark, the light we find.
Whispers grow into a song,
In the twilight, we are strong.

Serpentine Shadows on the River's Edge

Beneath the boughs, the shadows twist,
Serpentine forms through mist persist.
On the river's shimmering face,
Secrets hide in darkened grace.

Silent ripples gently sigh,
Echoes of the night passing by.
Where the willows weep and sway,
Lies the magic of the day.

Coolness breathes in whispers low,
Touching dreams that ebb and flow.
Through the dusk, the shadows flick,
Weaving tales both strange and quick.

On the banks, the twilight bends,
Magic follows where it wends.
Serpentine dance of light and shade,
Like a story softly laid.

Wanderers pause, hearts ablaze,
Caught within this winding maze.
In shadows deep, the truth resides,
By the river, where time slides.

Ashen Breeze in the Twilight Glow

In the evening's soft embrace,
An ashen breeze begins its race.
Carrying whispers from afar,
Guiding hearts like a distant star.

Through the trees, the branches sigh,
In this moment, time is nigh.
Golden hues kiss the earth,
Rounding corners of rebirth.

Fleeting shadows mar the light,
As the day gives in to night.
Every breath a gentle sigh,
While the embers fade and die.

Twilight's magic, rich and sweet,
Wrapped in dreams from head to feet.
In the hush of fading glow,
Time slows down, as rivers flow.

Feel the pulse of nature's song,
In this bond, we all belong.
Ashen breezes tell the tales,
Of the night to which it sails.

Twilight Reflections in Broken Glass

In twilight soft, the shadows play,
A dance of light at end of day.
The glass reflects a fading glow,
Whispers of dreams that ebb and flow.

Each crack a tale of days long past,
A shimmering echo, memories cast.
The colors swirl in fragile guise,
Secrets held in silent sighs.

Beneath the stars, the quiet hum,
Of life that pulses, yet feels numb.
Fragments twinkle, hopes once bright,
Now scattered shards in growing night.

Through splintered visions, visions meld,
The heart remembers, stories held.
In twilight's grasp, there's magic still,
A fragile world, both cold and warm.

Thus in the glass, we find our truth,
Within the whispers of fleeting youth.
Our twilight dances, ever last,
Reflections caught in moments passed.

Light and Shadow on the Winding Path

A winding path through ancient trees,
Where sunlight filters, soft as breeze.
The play of shadows, light fills space,
A secret journey, a hidden place.

Each step unfolds a tale untold,
Connecting hearts, both young and old.
The laughter echoes through the air,
A tapestry of time laid bare.

With every curve, the world could change,
An unseen magic, vast and strange.
In light and dark, we seek to find,
The whispers of the heart and mind.

Underneath the painted skies,
We chase the dreams that never die.
The winding path, both swift and slow,
Guides us to where the wild winds blow.

In shadows deep, we find our way,
Emerging from the end of day.
With every turn, a choice is made,
A journey bright, through light and shade.

Cinematic Haze Over Fluid Memories

In cinema's glow, we drift away,
Past flickering scenes of yesterday.
A hazy frame where dreams reside,
Fluid moments, our hearts confide.

Each whisper casts a shimmering gleam,
Holding fast to a fleeting dream.
The silver screen, a magical place,
Where memories blend, time's soft embrace.

Through frames of gold and moments rare,
We journey back, with gentle care.
Each laugh and tear, a precious hold,
The tales of life, both new and old.

In hazy depths, reflections rise,
A vivid dance beneath the skies.
The cinematic haze encircles wide,
Guiding us on this joyful ride.

In every scene, a spark ignites,
As fluid memories take to flight.
In silver shimmer, our hearts ignite,
In the cinematic glow of night.

Fractured Gleams on Forgotten Waters

Upon the lake, where shadows glide,
Forgotten waters, secrets hide.
Fractured gleams of silver bright,
A haunting vision in the night.

The ripples tell of days gone by,
Whispers carried on the sigh.
Reflected dreams on sunset's hue,
Lost illusions waiting for you.

In every wave, a story wakes,
Of treasures deep, the heart remakes.
We glimpse the past in twilight's spell,
In fractured light, the echoes dwell.

As darkness gathers 'round the shore,
The waters pulse with dreams of yore.
Forgotten glimmers, tales to weave,
In quiet moments, we believe.

Through fractured gleams, we find our way,
The waters call, with soft decay.
In stillness holds the heart's desire,
As memories dance in twilight's fire.

Flickers Beneath the Mournful Clouds

In twilight's grip, where shadows weave,
A whisper calls, a tale to grieve.
The stars glance down, with tender light,
As dreams take wing, in darkest night.

Beneath the weight of sorrowed skies,
The heart finds peace, as hope still flies.
A flicker bright, a beacon's gleam,
In night's embrace, we dare to dream.

Aerial Trails of Fickle Spirits

Above the trees where starlings dance,
Fickle spirits sway in trance.
They spin their tales on winds so light,
A symphony of day and night.

With laughter sweet, they flit and play,
Chasing shadows of the day.
In every gust, their secrets speak,
A fleeting smile, a gentle peek.

Soothing the Weary Hearth

Beneath the eaves, the fire glows,
A warm embrace, where comfort grows.
With crackling logs, the shadows dance,
A song of peace, a whispered chance.

The embers hum, a lullaby,
To weary souls that wander nigh.
In corners dim, where dreams reside,
The hearth's soft glow, a tender guide.

Where the Cinders Flutter

In ashes deep, where memories lie,
Cinders flutter in the sky.
Each spark a wish, a fleeting glance,
Of moments lost, in certain chance.

They whisper tales of days gone by,
In twilight's kiss, they softly sigh.
With every breath, the past ignites,
A dance of shadows, a swirl of lights.

Sighs of the Flame-kissed Atmosphere

In twilight's soft embrace we sit,
The fire dances with a gentle wit.
Whispers curl from embers bright,
Carrying tales into the night.

Stars peek through a smoky shroud,
Their glimmer hidden in a cloud.
The twilight sighs beneath our gaze,
As time weaves magic in its haze.

A warmth surrounds like a woven lace,
Drawing hearts to a sacred space.
With each flicker, dreams ignite,
Reflecting hopes in golden light.

Ashes settle in a sweet refrain,
Every spark a hint of pain.
Yet laughter lingers, soft and clear,
In this night, we hold our dear.

Together we share our whispered fears,
In the glow, our laughter cheers.
The flame, a witness to our plight,
As shadows dance in soft moonlight.

Dusk's Embrace on Grit and Flame

Dusk descends with velvet grace,
Painting shadows, taking space.
The grit we tread on whispers low,
While sparks ignite in evening's glow.

With every breath the night unfolds,
Tales of valor and of old.
Flame-kissed air stirs weary minds,
Binding paths that fate unwinds.

In the heart of fire, secrets churn,
Lessons taught and hard-earned.
With moonlight weaving through the trees,
A symphony upon the breeze.

Cinders fly to greet the stars,
Echoes tremble from afar.
A dance of shadows on the hill,
Wrapping the night in calm, until

All hearts are drawn to flickering light,
Seeking comfort through the night.
Together found in shimmering flame,
The dusk's embrace will hold our name.

Soliloquy of the Sooty Veil

Beneath the sooty veil we hide,
With secrets kept so deeply tied.
In silence, ghosts of dreams take flight,
Yearning to escape the night.

The shadows weave a tale so grand,
Of whispered hopes and gentle hand.
Embers murmur in the dark,
Catching whispers, striking spark.

Yet in the chill, a warmth remains,
Embracing all our silent pains.
With every flicker, echoes bold,
A story of the brave retold.

Veils of soot can't hide the light,
For within the shadow dwells the fight.
Each heartbeat thrums against the hush,
As dreams emerge from midnight's crush.

In solitude, the voices blend,
A symphony that will not end.
Through the darkness, we shall prevail,
Bound together beyond the veil.

The Lament of the Fiery Gale

A tempest roars in fiery breath,
Spanning the land like a dance with death.
Flames twist and turn, a wild waltz,
As whispers claim the night and pulse.

The gale carries tales of despair,
Of those who yearned for hearts laid bare.
In every gust, a chapter torn,
In every spark, a hope reborn.

Yet from the ashes, seeds will grow,
An ember's warmth, a gentle glow.
Through gusts of flame, they rise anew,
Survivors forged from trials few.

As night surrenders to breaks of dawn,
The fiery gale shifts, and life moves on.
No longer lost amidst the strife,
Bold new spirits embrace the life.

Though storms may wail their mournful song,
We find our strength; we all belong.
With every breath, the gale will say,
We are the fire that lights the way.

Reverberations from the Abyss

In shadows where the echoes play,
The whispers of the lost decay.
Each heartbeat thrums like distant drums,
A serenade where darkness hums.

From depths unseen, they start to rise,
A symphony of silent sighs.
The ancient tales of sorrow sing,
Like phantom hands on ghostly string.

Through hollow voids where light is faint,
The echoes dance, a haunting paint.
With every breath of night's embrace,
We feel the pulse of time and space.

Awake the dreams, let shadows weave,
A tapestry of those who grieve.
For every whisper forged in night,
Bears witness to the fading light.

So linger long in muted fear,
And hold the echoes ever near.
For in the dark, the truth persists,
As echoes whisper, "We exist."

Celestial Whirlpools of Transience

In cosmic dance, the stars collide,
In fleeting moments, hopes abide.
A swirling mist of time and space,
A carousel of dreams we chase.

Through nebulous paths, the shadows twine,
As starlight weaves through threads divine.
Each breath a spark, a burst of flame,
Yet nothing holds, and all's the same.

With every glance at distant skies,
We ponder fate and whispered lies.
In shapes of light, the stories flow,
Yet truth is lost where shadows glow.

The universe a fleeting tide,
With gentle tug where moments bide.
In swirling mists of dark and gold,
We find the warmth of tales retold.

So ride the waves, let starlight guide,
Through whirlpools vast, let dreams abide.
For in this dance of bright unknown,
We find the seeds of love we've sown.

Lament of the Starlit Torrents

The river flows with wishes lost,
A stream of dreams at silvered cost.
With every drop, a tale unfolds,
Of hearts once warm, now turned to cold.

Above, the stars in silence weep,
Guarding secrets that they keep.
In torrents wild, the currents sigh,
As echoes fade, and lovers cry.

The moonlit path, a transient shore,
Where shadows dance and spirits soar.
Each ripple holds the weight of night,
A lament dressed in shimmering light.

Through darkened skies, the memories wail,
Of joy entwined with sorrow's trail.
Yet still the river calls our name,
A haunting echo, a flickering flame.

So sail the currents, brave the night,
Embrace the grief, embrace the light.
For in the flow of time's embrace,
We find the love that knows no space.

Translucent Whispers Behind the Currents

In water's heart, where stillness lies,
The secrets weave, a quilt of sighs.
Translucent whispers gently flow,
Through currents soft, where shadows grow.

Beneath the veil, the echoes creep,
In silken threads, the silence deep.
A tapestry of dreams and fears,
While laughter's ghost still lingers near.

The tides of time, they ebb and swell,
Each pulse a story, each drop a spell.
We hear the tales of bygone lands,
Where spirit dances, walks by hands.

As rivers share their fleeting grace,
The past invites us to embrace.
With every breath, the world ignites,
In whispers shared on starry nights.

So listen close to waters' sigh,
For in the depth, we cannot lie.
The current's song holds truth profound,
In translucent whispers, we are found.

Flickering Haze Beneath the Shimmering Stars

In the dusk, a glow takes flight,
Whispers weave through the night.
Beneath the stars, dreams ignite,
Magic dances, pure delight.

Shadows play on silver beams,
Crickets hum in gentle themes.
Winds of wonder softly swirl,
In this realm, our fates unfurl.

Eyes like lanterns, bright and wide,
Hoping, wishing, hearts collide.
In the haze, time slips away,
Lost in dreams, we long to stay.

Murmurs rise from fields of gold,
Tales of love and vows retold.
The flickering lights whisper low,
Secrets only night can know.

As the night begins to fade,
Laughter echoing, serenade.
Beneath the stars, we find our place,
In the haze, time's sweet embrace.

Timeless Ripples on the Water's Skin

Glimmers dance like waltzing dreams,
Beneath the moon, the water gleams.
A gentle wave, a tender sigh,
Where time drifts slowly, floating by.

Peering deep in the mirrored glow,
Secrets held within the flow.
Timeless whispers, ages past,
Reflections of shadows cast.

Stone by stone, the pathway fades,
Footsteps light where love cascades.
Ripples pulse, a heartbeat's tune,
Revealing stories sung to the moon.

Beneath the willow's soft embrace,
Time suspends, a tranquil grace.
In this stillness, life is spun,
Whispers shared and dreams begun.

As stars twinkle in muted haze,
We lose ourselves in the night's gaze.
Every ripple, a tale unfolds,
On water's skin, the heart beholds.

Murmurs of the Twilight Tide

Softly hums the evening breeze,
Cards of fate, the world to tease.
Twilight sprawls in hues so sweet,
Where day and night so tenderly meet.

Tides of whispers gently crash,
Echoing dreams in a fleeting flash.
Moonlit secrets, softly shared,
Murmurs of love, hearts laid bare.

The shore cradles each embrace,
Waves caress, a tender grace.
In the rhythm, we find our rhyme,
Bathed in echoes of ageless time.

Stars ignite, a velvet sweep,
In twilight's arms, we safely leap.
Wanderlust beneath the sky,
Where every moment dares to fly.

As dreams dissolve with morning's light,
We hold the magic of the night.
In twilight's tide, we learn to see,
The whispers of eternity.

Enigma of the Stillness Beneath

In quiet depths where silence sings,
The stillness weaves its ancient strings.
Every heartbeat, a secret kept,
In shadows cast where echoes crept.

Beneath the surface, worlds collide,
Mysteries coil where hopes reside.
Fathomless dreams in silence spin,
Whispering tales of what has been.

Light and dark in a dance so bold,
Stories shimmer, waiting to be told.
The enigma swells like a toothless grin,
In the locket where time begins.

Flashes of laughter, cries of wall,
Within this stillness, we hear it all.
Waves of longing, breaths entwined,
In the hush, our souls aligned.

As dawn approaches, whispers fade,
Leaving footprints, memories made.
In the stillness, we understand,
Life's enigma, vast and grand.

Specters of the Blazing Tides

In shadows cast by moonlit waves,
The specters dance, the ocean braves.
With whispers soft, on silver sand,
They weave their tales, both bright and grand.

Their laughter twirls through night's embrace,
While tides swirl round in wild, fierce grace.
From depths unseen, they rise and swell,
Carrying secrets, a haunting spell.

The flames reflected on the shore,
In flickering light, they seem to soar.
Against the storms of time, they fight,
Each wave a memory, lost to night.

Yet as the dawn begins to break,
The specters fade with each heartache.
Gone with the tide, they drift away,
In whispered winds that softly play.

But linger still, their tales remain,
In every wave, love and pain.
A world awash with dreams untold,
Through blazing tides, their hearts unfold.

Songs of the Flickering Glow

In candlelight, the stories gleam,
Each flickering flame a whispered dream.
They dance in shadows, soft and low,
With notes that linger, hearts aglow.

Through winding halls of past's embrace,
The echoes of laughter we can trace.
With every flicker, time stands still,
A magic fills the air, a thrill.

The songs of old, in tender tune,
Beneath the watchful, silver moon.
They flutter soft like summer's breeze,
In gentle sighs, the soul finds ease.

With every echo, memories glow,
In whispered tales of love we know.
Through joys and sorrows, we remain,
In light's embrace, both loss and gain.

So let the flicker guide our way,
As shadows dance and dreams hold sway.
In songs of warmth, our hearts will find,
The flickering glow that leaves us blind.

Serpents of the Tempestuous Air

In tempest's breath, the serpents glide,
Through billowing clouds, they twist and slide.
With eyes of storm and wings of night,
They carve the darkness, fierce and bright.

A howling call, like thunder's roar,
They spiral high, through sky they soar.
Each flick of tail ignites the sky,
A dance of chaos, wild and spry.

Across the heavens, tales are spun,
Of battles lost and victories won.
With every tempest, more they strive,
In swirling gales, they come alive.

Yet peace may follow stormy flight,
As dawn awakes with softest light.
The serpents whisper, secrets bare,
A lullaby within the air.

So let the winds tell tales anew,
Of tempest's dance and skies so blue.
In every breath, a storm we dare,
With serpents weaving through the air.

Manifest of the Wraith-like Drift

A wraith-like drift in twilight's hue,
Through veils of mist, they float anew.
In silence deep, they weave their paths,
With shadows kissed by evening's baths.

Their forms like whispers, softly glide,
Through dreams and realms where hearts abide.
A gentle touch, a fleeting grace,
In every glance, a lost embrace.

As stardust mingles with the night,
They dance in circles, pure delight.
From dusk till dawn, they come alive,
In every heart, their spirits strive.

With echoes faint, they make their calls,
Through ancient woods and crumbling halls.
In twilight's glow, they find their rest,
In memories kept, forever blessed.

So linger close, in softest dream,
Where wraiths abound and moonbeams gleam.
In drifting forms, our hearts will lift,
To join the dance in wraith-like drift.

Veils of the Fuming Dawn

In shades of gray, the day breaks forth,
Whispers of light, a glimmering mirth.
With shadows long, the secrets sigh,
Veils of the fuming dawn drift by.

A dance of mist in the morning air,
Each drop of dew, a whispered prayer.
With tendrils soft, it cloaks the earth,
Embracing all with gentle girth.

The sun awakes with a golden eye,
Chasing the sorrows of night's goodbye.
As warmth envelops the waking trees,
Life stirs anew with the morning breeze.

A promise lies in the pastel sky,
Dreams emerge as the world complies.
Hope glimmers bright, like a star reborn,
Amidst the veils of the fuming dawn.

With every pulse, the heartbeat swells,
In whispered tales, the universe dwells.
And so we greet, with minds set free,
The painted dawn and all it can be.

Through the Haze of the Burnt Night

Through the haze of the burnt night sky,
Flickering embers still linger nearby.
Shadows conspire in the pale moonlight,
Dreamers and schemers take flight tonight.

Each whispered word a silken thread,
Woven with tales of the sleeping dead.
In corners dark where secrets play,
The silence hums, and spirits sway.

Glimmers of truth twinkle on high,
Stars hold the stories we dare not cry.
The full moon watches as visions blaze,
And we dance amidst the smoky haze.

With every heartbeat, the night unfolds,
A kaleidoscope of truths retold.
In shadows deep, we find delight,
Through the haze of the burnt night.

But in the embers, a promise glows,
Of dawn's return and the warmth it sows.
So revel in darkness, let dreams ignite,
For all shall awaken with morning's light.

Tales from the Searing Veil

In the heart of night, where shadows creep,
Lies a world of whispers, secrets we keep.
Through the searing veil, our truths appear,
In flickers of light, we face our fear.

With tales entwined, each moment breathes,
A tapestry woven with shadows and leaves.
They speak of journeys taken in haze,
Through the labyrinth of forgotten days.

Glimmers of hope hide in every word,
Painted in hues that cannot be heard.
The heart listens close, as night unveils,
The hidden stories from the searing veils.

A spark ignites and the flame responds,
Carving new paths like fabled wands.
In echoes of laughter, and distant calls,
Tales of resilience, our spirit enthralls.

So gather around as the shadows blend,
In the warmth of the stories that never end.
Through the darkened land where our fate entails,
We find our strength from the searing veils.

Ashes Lifted by the Zephyr

As ashes rise on the gentle wind,
Carried away where the dreams have sinned.
They twirl and spin in the soft twilight,
Like whispers of souls lost in their flight.

The zephyr calls with a playful tease,
A brush of warmth in the evening breeze.
With tender grace, it lifts our fears,
Transforming sorrow, like hidden cheers.

In the twilight glow, the embers gleam,
Flickers of hope in a wistful dream.
A canvas painted, with colors vast,
Where future blends with the echoing past.

Each breath a memory, each sigh a tale,
As freedom dances with the whispering gale.
With time unbound, we rise anew,
Ashes lifted by the zephyr's cue.

So let them soar, those fragments lost,
For every end holds its own cost.
In gentle winds, our spirits sail,
Transformed and free, through the zephyr's trail.

Reflections of the Day's Last Breath

Golden hues fade in the sky,
As shadows stretch and whisper by.
A gentle hush, the world inhales,
While stars prepare their silver trails.

In the twilight's soft embrace,
The day concedes its fleeting grace.
Colors blend, and silence sings,
As night unfurls its velvet wings.

Luminous orbs begin to rise,
Winking softly from painted skies.
In pondered thoughts that weave and twine,
Memories glimmer, pure and divine.

The breeze carries tales untold,
Of whispered secrets, young and old.
Each breath a tale, each sigh a song,
As night descends where hearts belong.

Wrapped in dreams so calm and deep,
The world drifts softly into sleep.
With every heartbeat of the night,
Reflections dance in gentle light.

Quicksilver Dreams Beneath the Surface

In the depths where shadows blend,
Quicksilver dreams, they twist and spend.
Rippling visions, whispers sing,
In aquatic realms, the phantoms cling.

Beneath the waves, a world concealed,
Where secrets dwell, and fate is sealed.
Ethereal shapes in silver glide,
Through currents swirling, they abide.

Fragments of light weave through the swell,
In silent stories only time can tell.
Mirrored echoes of thoughts unspoken,
In these depths, a spell is broken.

Awash in hues of blue and green,
Beneath the moon's soft, watchful sheen.
Chasing dreams that dare to dive,
In this quiet, they come alive.

With every ripple, questions rise,
In the stillness, truth belies.
Quicksilver dreams in currents flow,
Guiding hearts where few can go.

Chronicles of Currents in Subtle Haze

Currents whisper through the leaves,
Tales of time in subtle eves.
A foggy breath enfolds the ground,
Where echoes of the past resound.

Drifting hopes on twilight's breeze,
Chronicles told through swaying trees.
In the mist, the stories blend,
Where memories find no clear end.

An endless stream of dreams awaits,
In hushed exchange with destiny's fates.
Each ripple dances, soft and slow,
Guiding souls where feelings grow.

Through smoky veils the shadows dart,
Carrying whispers that touch the heart.
Subtle hues in soft embrace,
Hold the threads of time and space.

With every pulse of twilight's grace,
Currents churn in a timeless race.
In this haze, the world aligns,
And in its rhythm, magic shines.

Ethereal Echoes Above the Still Waters

Beneath the glow of moonlit beams,
Ethereal echoes dance in dreams.
On still waters, reflections sway,
As night unfolds its soft ballet.

Ripples trace a melody sweet,
In the silence, the heart's quick beat.
Echoes drift through twilight's song,
Where whispered thoughts can't help but long.

The stars above in quiet gleam,
Share secrets spun from midnight's dream.
Each twinkle holds a wish untold,
In the depths of shadows, bright and bold.

The night breathes softly, calm and deep,
While waters wake from quiet sleep.
Ethereal voices, sweet and clear,
Invite the dreamers to draw near.

In rapture caught, the heart takes flight,
Above still waters, life ignites.
With every echo, hope renews,
In the stillness, nothing to lose.

Echoes Beneath a Fading Sky

In twilight's grip, the shadows play,
Whispers of dreams, drifting away.
A soft sigh lingers, hope takes flight,
Chasing the stars that melt in the night.

The moon hangs low, a silver seam,
Carving the silence, threading a dream.
Each heartbeat echoes, lost in the vast,
Beneath the fading sky, shadows are cast.

Winds tell secrets of where we roam,
While twilight beckons us gently home.
With every breath, the dusk unfolds,
Tales of the past, in silence told.

Veils of the night, softly unfurl,
Glimmers of magic in a whirling swirl.
Faded laughter that pierces the gloom,
Awakening wonders in the twilight bloom.

So linger here, where dreams reside,
In echoes beneath the sky's last tide.
Each moment fleeting, yet bold and bright,
Our stories entwined in the fading light.

Shimmering Veils of Lost Horizons

On the edge of dawn, where shadows blend,
Light dances freely, no need to mend.
Illusions shimmer, horizons bend,
In a world where every path seems to end.

Golden threads weave through the air,
Capturing visions, vibrant and rare.
With whispers of silk, they narrate the past,
In shimmering veils, lost dreams are cast.

Misty outlines of a world not shown,
Promises linger, yet barely known.
Time treads softly, a vigilant guide,
As shimmering veils of dreams reside.

In every heartbeat, a story waits,
Beneath the surface, the mystery states.
With every glance, the horizons wane,
Yet beauty whispers, it'll rise again.

So let the colors embrace the day,
As shimmering veils lead dreams away.
To realms where wonder forever reigns,
And lost horizons run with the rains.

Mirage of Dusk on Silver Streams

In twilight's breath, the waters gleam,
A mirage dances, a haunting dream.
Silver ripples weave through the night,
Casting reflections of fading light.

The whispers of dusk caress the shore,
Tales of existence, forgotten lore.
As shadows embrace the softly flowing,
Wonders awaken, all gently glowing.

Time flies slowly, in the evening's song,
Where every ripple feels like a throng.
The essence of twilight, sweet and sublime,
Delivers a heartbeat that mirrors time.

A tapestry spun with threads of the past,
In a world where dreams and reality cast.
Reflections shimmer beneath the sky's seam,
A mirage of dusk on silver streams.

So linger a moment, breathe in the night,
With each silver glance, the stars feel right.
For in the dusk, where sorrows gleam,
The heart finds its solace, lost in the dream.

Embers of Memory in the Glistening Air

In the twilight glow, embers ignite,
Flickering stories, soft as the night.
Whispers of days wrapped in the mist,
Where memories linger, tenderly kissed.

A curtain of stars twinkles above,
Each spark a moment, a whisper of love.
In the glistening air, time holds its breath,
Rekindling flames that dance against death.

The echoes of laughter, a soft refrain,
Reminding us gently of joy and of pain.
With each drifting ember, a tale comes clear,
Of moments once sacred, forever held dear.

Beneath the heavens, where wishes are sown,
Embers of memory softly have grown.
Through glistening air, they weave and entwine,
In the fabric of life, your heart aligns.

So gather these moments, let them replay,
For embers of memory guide us each day.
In the glow of the night, find solace and cheer,
In the sweet, glistening air, we hold all we hold dear.

Ripples of Forgotten Flames

In shadows of embers, whispers glide,
Old memories flicker, and dreams abide.
Time's gentle touch on forgotten fray,
As echoes of fire dance and sway.

Lost in the haze of the night's embrace,
The remnants of warmth leave a trace.
A flicker, a spark, in twilight's game,
Igniting the heart, never the same.

Once bold and bright, now dull and weak,
The language of silence begins to speak.
Yet, through the dark, the embers fight,
To weave a tale of enduring light.

With every ripple, new stories bloom,
In the quiet of night, dispelling gloom.
Through ashes and time, we recall,
The flames of the past that beckon us all.

In the distance, a glow begins to rise,
Painting the sky with fiery ties.
A phoenix awakens, its spirit aflame,
In ripples of hope, never the same.

Rise of the Searing Mist

A shroud of the morning, thick and gray,
Hides secrets and shadows, keeps them at bay.
With tendrils that curl, it starts to creep,
Over fields where lost dreams softly weep.

It whispers of stories long left untold,
Of battles and glories, of hearts gone cold.
Yet within the mist, there's warmth to find,
A spark of the past that lingers behind.

As daybreak approaches, the mist takes flight,
Glinting with hints of a golden light.
Each drop of dew, a treasure concealed,
Mirroring dreams that fate has revealed.

With every dawn, the mist starts to fade,
Leaving traces of magic, a delicate braid.
New paths emerge as the vision expands,
A journey reborn in unseen lands.

The rise of the mist, a vivid embrace,
Invites us to wander, to seek, to trace.
In the heart of the fog, there's beauty to thrill,
The searing touch of wonder we feel.

Breath of the Sulfurous Morn

In a land where the mountains breathe steam,
The air thick with echoes, both fierce and serene.
Sulfurous whispers waft on the breeze,
Nature's own lullaby, meant to appease.

Awakening worlds where darkness once lay,
New life emerges, in vibrant display.
With each halting step, the ground starts to steer,
A dance of the minerals, sharp yet clear.

The scent of the earth, like memories lost,
Reminds us of journeys, of paths we crossed.
Each breath, a reminder, both potent and bold,
Of secrets unveiled, and wonders retold.

Through valleys of echoes, the canyons reply,
As whispers of danger and beauty entwine.
In the heart of the morn, we'll seek and explore,
The breath of the land, forever we'll adore.

In the embrace of the dawn, let us unite,
Raise voices together, shaping the night.
For in every sulfurous morn that we greet,
Lies the pulse of the earth, alive and complete.

Echoes in the Charred Horizon

Burnt skies stretch wide, where shadows have played,
Fragments of twilight in smoky cascade.
The horizon, a canvas of muted despair,
Echoes the stories of love lost in air.

There, amidst fractals of flickering light,
Memories linger, both haunting and bright.
A journey through ashes, where spirits reside,
Offering solace to those who confide.

Above the charred earth, where silence was sown,
The whispers of past lives can still be known.
Each gust of the wind carries tales untold,
Of trials endured and of hearts turned bold.

In twilight's embrace, as the dusk starts to fall,
The horizon pulses, an eternal call.
An echo of strength in the face of defeat,
Resilience blooms, a victory sweet.

Onward we tread, through the remnants of flame,
Witnessing shadows that whisper our name.
For in every echo, a lesson will rise,
In the charred horizon, new hope ever lies.

Reflections of a Forgotten Flame

In shadows deep, where memories lie,
A flicker dims beneath the sky.
Echoes call from the hearth so warm,
A blaze once bright, now weathered, worn.

The hearth is cold, yet whispers soar,
Of stories told, of yesterdays lore.
Ghostly figures dance in the night,
Reflecting dreams in the pale moonlight.

The flick of a flame, a moment's grace,
Now but a sigh, a fleeting trace.
In every heart, a spark remains,
Of loved ones lost, of joyful gains.

Life's currents churn, like leaves in fall,
In the silence deep, we hear their call.
Each ember flickers, a pulse of time,
In the quietude, a whispered rhyme.

Yet in the dark, the night unfolds,
A silent warmth that softly hold.
Reflections of love in every spark,
A forgotten flame ignites the dark.

Threads of Smoke and Whispered Dreams

In the twilight hour, where shadows blend,
Threads of smoke rise, with stories to send.
Whispers twine in the cooling air,
Reflections caught in a dreamer's stare.

From silvered lips, the secrets flow,
In moonlit dances, where dreams bestow.
A tapestry spun from hopes and fears,
Each thread a journey, soaked in tears.

A cottage lingers on a misty glade,
With tales of yore that time has laid.
The lanterns glow like stars above,
Igniting passion, igniting love.

With every wish cast on whispered breath,
The threads entwined defy even death.
For in their weaving, magic wakes,
In the chance of dreams, the heart it takes.

So chase the wisps as they softly fade,
In the depths of night, a serenade.
Threads of smoke and dreams entwine,
In the quiet embrace, our souls align.

Secrets Flowing From Hidden Springs

From stony lips, the water flows,
Where sunlight dances, nobody knows.
Secrets hidden beneath the stone,
In twilight's grasp, they're left alone.

A sacred pool, where wishes pour,
Reflects the heavens, tales of yore.
Each droplet glimmers with thoughts unfurled,
In whispers soft, they shape the world.

With every ripple, a story wakes,
Of longing hearts and boundless stakes.
In shrouded depths, the truths reside,
Flowing like currents, with hope as guide.

Among the leaves, the breezes hum,
As from the depths, secrets come.
From hidden springs, our dreams suspended,
In waters clear, the past is blended.

Let nature's voice, in silence sing,
Unveil the joy that spring can bring.
In every drop, a life anew,
Secrets flowing, pure and true.

Wraiths Dancing on the Glassy Surface

Beneath the moon, on waters still,
Wraiths emerge, as shadows thrill.
In silent grace, they twirl around,
On the glassy surface, without a sound.

Their tales unfold in the night so deep,
Through swirling mists, while mortals sleep.
Each flicker of light, a ghostly kiss,
In the dance of wraiths, we find our bliss.

With spirits whispered on the breeze,
They draw us close, in twilight tease.
Every flutter sends a spark,
A stirring haiku in the dark.

They weave a world of haunting dreams,
Where time dissolves and silence gleams.
In mirrored depths, our souls take flight,
Wraiths dancing in the depth of night.

Embrace the chill as shadows play,
In swirling moonlight, let fears decay.
For on that surface, pure and bright,
Wraiths dance with us, lost in the light.

Cascading Echoes of Lost Fires

In the darkened woods, whispers glide,
Ghosts from the embers where dreams reside.
Flickering shadows weave tales untold,
Echoes of laughter, both warm and cold.

The night air thick with secrets and sighs,
Stars twinkle softly as time gently flies.
Cinders of passion now drift in the breeze,
Carrying memories with effortless ease.

Once were the moments that sparked in the night,
Now doused in shadows beyond our sight.
Yet still the heart holds a radiant flame,
Nurturing hope in the flickering game.

With every whisper, a heartbeat is shared,
In the tapestry woven, we're never scared.
For even in silence, their stories survive,
Cascading echoes that keep dreams alive.

Each flame lost to time has a lesson to give,
In the dance of the embers, remember to live.
For in every whisper, in every sigh,
Lies the promise of love that will never die.

Allure of the Undercurrent's Breath

Beneath the surface, a world stirs slow,
Where secrets of water and shadow flow.
Currents weaving tales as they twist and turn,
In each gentle pool, new passions burn.

The darkened depths hold enchantments vast,
Mirrors reflect futures and echoes of past.
With every ripple, a whisper reveals,
The allure of dreams that the heart conceals.

As glimmers of light dance on velvet blue,
The undercurrent breathes, inviting you.
It beckons with secrets, it pulls with the tide,
Drawing you near to the wonders inside.

With each brimming wave, possibilities rise,
An unseen world beneath silver skies.
Let go of the shore, let curiosity lead,
For the depths are alive with the hopes that we need.

In silence, the waters will sing you a song,
Of journeys and wishes that all can belong.
So dive into magic where mysteries play,
Embrace the allure of the undulating sway.

Flames Lost in the Weave of Time

In the flicker of lanterns, stories ignite,
Woven through ages, bright against the night.
Threads of adventure, both tangled and fine,
We hold them close as we search for the sign.

Dancing through echoes of laughter and tears,
The flames of our past light the shadows of years.
With each tender flame, a memory stirs,
Sparks from the hearth where the heart gently purrs.

But time is a thief in its never-ending chase,
Taking our moments, yet leaving a trace.
We grasp at the fire, yet it slips from our hands,
The tapestry shifts, as the universe plans.

Yet within the weave, there's a glittering thread,
Of dreams unforgotten and words left unsaid.
For even when flames dance away from our gaze,
The light from their glow we will always raise.

So cherish the warmth of the fires we keep,
In the heart of the night, where our spirits leap.
For though they may fade, and the embers may tire,
The weave of our lives forever burns higher.

Mysteries Behind the Shifting Mists

Through the shroud of fog, where shadows reside,
Lies a world of wonders that dreams cannot hide.
The mist curls and sways, veiling the way,
Inviting the curious to wander and stay.

In the whispers of twilight, secrets unfold,
Stories entwined as the night becomes bold.
Each step into stillness, a riddle unfurls,
As pathways are drawn in soft, swirling pearls.

Not all that glimmers in twilight's embrace,
Holds the truths hidden in time and space.
For some things are fleeting, like breath on a glass,
Mysterious moments that shimmer and pass.

Yet among the illusions, bright visions peep,
Shimmers of hope that awaken from sleep.
With every soft curl of the murmuring mist,
Lies an echo of dreams that we long to persist.

So heed the soft whispers that beckon you close,
In the heart of the fog, find the magic engrossed.
For behind every secret that hides from the light,
Are mysteries waiting to bloom in the night.

www.ingramcontent.com/pod-product-compliance
Ingram Content Group UK Ltd.
Pitfield, Milton Keynes, MK11 3LW, UK
UKHW021631200125
4187UKWH00003B/82

9 781805 633655